your Belly Bugs guide to happy eating

written by **David Bell** illustrated by **Martin Smith**

LITTLE RIVER

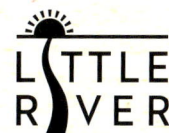

I'm **Billie Pickle.**
Gather round.
You won't believe what
I just found!

Hi!

Last night I had an awesome dream
In which I met a secret team...

When we've eaten all our lunch
It's our **Belly Bugs**' turn to munch.

They chomp the bits we can't digest
So we feel great and at our best.

When **Chewy Bug** chews veg or fruit
Out of his bum huge poos will shoot.

Those poos will keep **Rumbledom** green
And healthy like you've never seen.

Mushroom Control rises up high.
From there our Belly Bugs can spy
On what is happening down below
Like **Buglet** helpers on the go.

The Belly Deli stands next door
With food packed in on every floor.

It's where the food we've provided
Among our Bugs gets divided.

Chompy Bug
is her handyman.

Each day for him she has a plan.

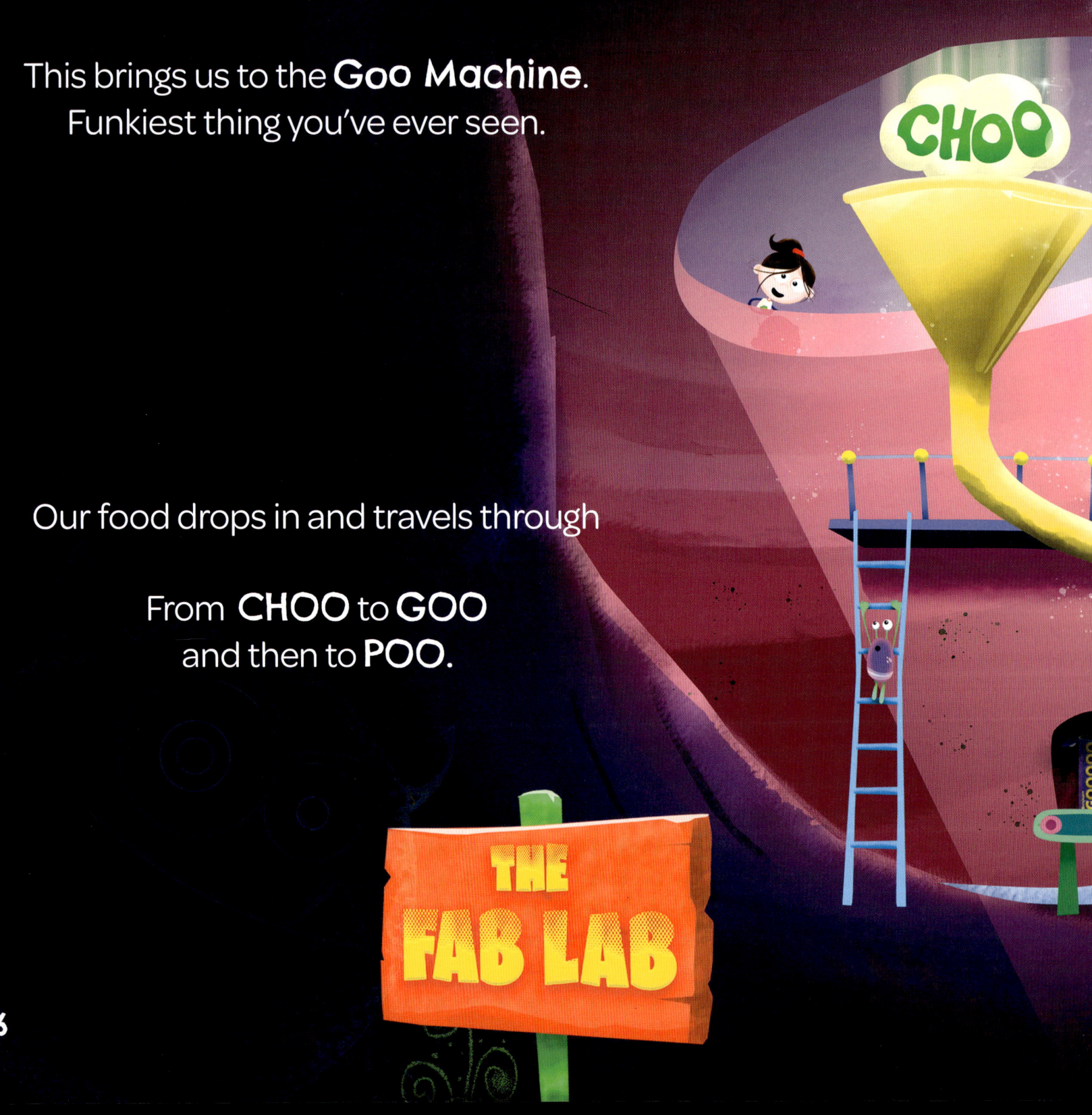

This brings us to the **Goo Machine**.
Funkiest thing you've ever seen.

Our food drops in and travels through

From **CHOO** to **GOO**
and then to **POO**.

THE FAB LAB

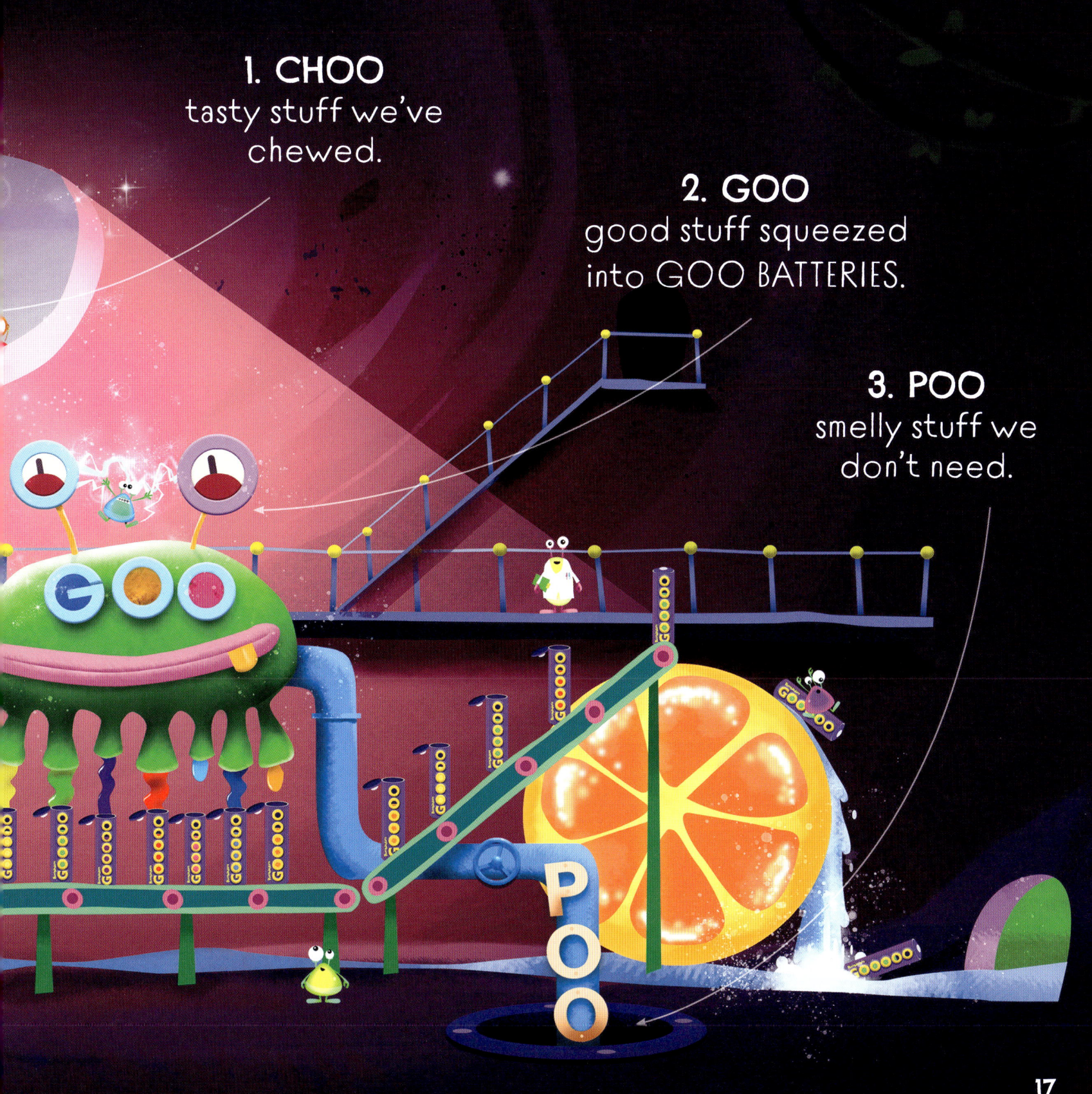

Happy Bug runs the **Rainbowtron**.

Puts batteries in and switches on.

It's where we get our energy
To run or play or climb a tree.

There is a lesson to be learned.
All our energy must be earned.

Eat rainbow colours that's the clue to fill your batteries up with Goo!

But Baddies invade

Rumbledom

Ultras
(in food made in factories)

Sugar Monsters
(in sweets & sugary drinks)

Junk Punks
(in fast food)

DOUBLE CHOCOLATE Cereal Flakes

Hidden in junk food, in they come.

22

Too many Baddies inside you

Soon will leave you feeling blue.

Here is the thing with cakes and sweets.

To feel tip-top, save them for treats.

Those **Belly Bugs** just know the score.
Our moods, feelings and so much more.

So 'butterflies in my tummy' is a message going up my Blube Tube when I'm excited, nervous or scared?

They're in the thick of things each day.
So 'Trust your gut!' like Gran would say.

This is a tale that never ends.
Belly Bugs are our closest friends.

When you get up, they get up too.
Ready to spend all day with you.

Before you eat, you should think twice. Would your **Belly Bugs** say it's nice?

What will you feed your **Belly Bugs today?**

Feed your Belly Bugs some fun!

Buglets

Pears

Melon

Peppers

Cooly Bug

Oranges

Apples

Spring onions

Happy Bug

Blueberries

Mushrooms

Bananas

Bashy Bug

Squash

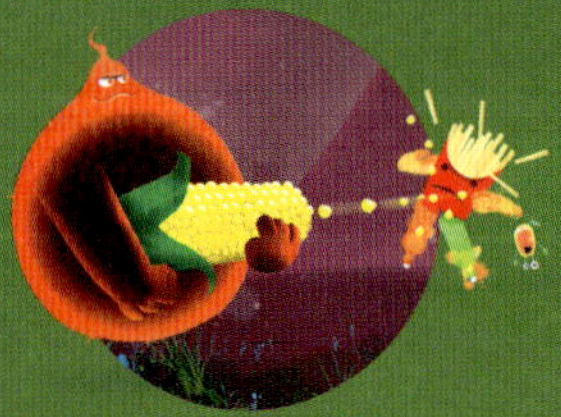
Sweetcorn

Sweet potato

Flicky Bug

Tomatoes

Kiwi

Broccoli